Thriver

My Journey Through Holocaust Nightmare to American Dream

Mendel Rosenberg

Photo credits: Page 25, Rimantas Lazdynas/Wikimedia Commons/Public Domain; Page 28, Stasys Ivanauskas/Wikimedia Commons/Public Domain; Page 32, Philipp P Egli/Wikimedia Commons/Public Domain; Page 34, Wojciech Strozyk/Alamy Stock Photo; Page 42, Tafkas/Wikimedia Commons/Public Domain;

Book design by LaVidaCo Communications

Printed in the United States of America

Library of Congress Control Number: 2019933546

ISBN: 978-1-950419-00-5

"For the dead and the living, we must bear witness. Not only are we responsible for the memories of the dead, we are responsible for what we do with those memories."

— Elie Wiesel

Table of Contents

Foreword

Ifirst met Mendel Rosenberg several years ago at a Holocaust film series that he and his wife, Sandy, were sponsoring. Afterward Mendel answered a few questions about his experiences, and I knew I wanted to hear more.

What I later learned was that it took Mendel quite some time before he could share his story. Mendel just celebrated his 90th birthday, and it wasn't until he was nearly 50 years old that he would speak to anyone about his experience as a Holocaust survivor. Even his children knew just a fraction of what he and his brother, mother, father, and grandmother had endured during World War II.

Mendel arrived with his mother in the U.S. in 1947. They were the only ones who had survived. Mendel very much wanted to put the horrific experience behind him. And, for the most part, he did. Mendel went from being a survivor to a thriver, marrying Sandy, a wonderful woman who he met in Youngstown, Ohio, raising a great family, and building a very successful business in St. Louis. It wasn't until the mid-1970s, that he began to share his story with others, the first time at a religious school. He told his story in a most understated way, which made it all the more powerful, and he began getting invitations to other religious schools and then to public schools. With the establishment of the Holocaust Museum & Learning Center in St. Louis 25 years ago, Mendel and other survivors had a special venue to tell their stories, which they have done dozens and dozens of times. Mendel also has generously shared his story with several oral historians.

But until now, Mendel had not put his remembrances on a page. When I asked him why, he said, "I don't think anyone would want to hear about it." My small role in this project is that I encouraged Mendel to do this because his story deserves to be told. I asked Dick Weiss to help him him share his story and this is the result.

Jerry Schlichter
January, 2019

Preface

Many people consider me a survivor. I am that to be sure.

I spent my teenage years with my grandmother, father, mother and brother in a ghetto the Nazis established and surrounded with barbed wire in my hometown of Siauliai, Lithuania. My father Simon was taken from us along with hundreds of other men on a summer day in 1941, made to dig a mass grave and then was murdered at the site. My grandmother, Ruth, died of a heart attack while we were in the ghetto.

In 1944, I was taken on a train with my mother, Recha, and older brother, Samuel, to Stutthof, a concentration camp in northern Poland. Later, Samuel and I were separated from our mother and taken to the Dachau concentration camp in southern Germany. Samuel, then 18, was beaten to death while on a work detail just a few months short of liberation. Only my mother and I survived the war. And she died at age 62 in 1957.

So I am the only one left to tell the story. And for a long time, I wanted to do almost anything other than share it. I like to think of myself as a thriver, not a survivor. In fact you could consider me the embodiment of the immigrant experience as articulated so beautifully by the poet Emma Lazarus, a Jew. She wrote the poem that can be found at the Statue of Liberty, which I saw for the first time in 1947 from the deck of a ship bringing me to America. I am sure that you -- and just about every American who has made it past the fifth grade -- know how it goes:

> *Give me your tired, your poor,*
> *Your huddled masses yearning to breathe free,*
> *The wretched refuse of your teeming shore.*
> *Send these, the homeless, tempest-tost to me,*
> *I lift my lamp beside the golden door!"*

That certainly was me. My mother and I arrived with pocket money and the clothes on our back. And, as mentioned, we had been tempest-tost to the utmost degree.

But starting almost from the very moment that I set foot in the United States of America, my life got better and better. To be sure, I encountered a few setbacks -- at one point I lost my job and had to start a new business practically from scratch. But compared to what I had been through, they were mere bumps in a road leading me to great happiness.

So for decades I had little interest in looking back at the suffering that I had endured. I was focused always on what lay ahead. I started a family and a business. Though my children knew that I had been through the Holocaust, I didn't want to burden them with sad tales. When it came to business, I never mentioned my background to associates, though they could tell from my accent that I was probably an immigrant.

Still, I could not leave my childhood experiences completely behind me. I suffered from nightmares for 30 years. And I also came to realize -- mostly from the examples set by other survivors -- that it was important to share my story so future generations could learn from it. This is not only so that a Holocaust would never happen again, but also so they could appreciate the blessings they enjoy in the "land of the free and the home of the brave."

So in 1978, I accepted an invitation to speak to a religious school class at Temple Israel in Creve Coeur, Mo., not far from my home. Later, I sat for interviews with Holocaust historians, most of which are recorded and can be found in various archives. In the 2000s, I spoke to many student groups across the St. Louis area, more than I can count.

My family also sponsors a film series devoted to Holocaust remembrance.

What I haven't done, until now, is to put my recollections into a book, something you can hold in your hand, and reflect upon as one only can with the written word. I have enlisted a writer, Richard H. Weiss, to help me with this effort.

I feel it is especially important to do this now. One reason, of course, is that I am not getting any younger. By the time you read this I will be 90 years old. Of the 72,000 survivors who came to the U.S., it is estimated that about 300 settled in the St. Louis area and fewer than 100 are living today.

But an even more important reason is the times in which we now live. I want people to learn from history, which I believe they have not. If they had, we would not have so much anti-immigrant feeling in our country today. We would not have so much rhetoric that pits one group of people against another. I find that people have not learned from the past. They make the same mistakes again and again.

I dedicate this work to my children, grandchildren, great-grandchildren, and to you and your descendants as well, so that they will appreciate their blessings and grow up in a world both prosperous and free.

Mendel Rosenberg
January, 2019

From left: Samuel, cousin Bluma, and Mendel

1

Roots

I wouldn't argue if you called my childhood idyllic. At the
time of my birth, September 18, 1928, my mother and
father were prospering. I was their second child. Samuel
came first in the spring of 1927.

We were both born in Königsberg, which was then part
of Germany, and is now known as Kaliningrad and part of
Russia. In the '20s, thousands of Jews lived there. Many
arrived anywhere from ten to 50 years earlier to escape
pogroms in Russia and many did quite well and did their
best to become patriotic citizens. According to one history,
more than 100,000 Jews served in the German Army during
World War I. Even so, as in Russia, Jews became subject to
discrimination and persecution after the war and they began
to leave for America, including some of my uncles and aunts.

I cannot tell you all that much about my grandparents
and great grandparents and whether they suffered through
pogroms or any form of oppression. I do know that my mother

was born in Tilzit, Germany, but went to school in Russia. She attended a university in Moscow and she learned to speak many eastern European languages, as well as French, and she was quite a Latin scholar as well.

I met my father's parents just once in 1937 when they were living in Latvia.

When I was a toddler, my mother, father, and maternal grandmother brought Samuel and me to Siauliai, Lithuania, about 165 miles northeast of Königsberg. Siauliai,was one of Lithuania's larger cities, and home to many Jews as well.

My father started a clothing store that he called Rosenberg's, with our nice apartment just a few blocks away.

Our store was on Vilniaus Gatve – that's the name of the street in Lithuanish. We had ready-made clothing for sale. We also displayed many bolts of cloth that shoppers could choose from and father had a small staff that would make garments for them.

Most of my boyhood was spent in this neighborhood except for the summers when we went to the seacoast.

As I said, those years were idyllic. But what we could not know as children was that Siauliai (and Königsberg as well) was caught in a vice between the Soviet Union and Germany. The 1920s and early 1930s would be remembered as a short period of relative independence and peace for families like ours.

When we arrived in Siauliai, the Jewish community numbered about six or seven thousand, about 20 percent of the city's population. Yet the Jews owned about half of the city's factories. I remember a tanning factory that employed hundreds of workers. This of course, put money in the pockets of everyone, some of which was spent at my family's store.

The Jewish community created trade organizations, started a hospital and, most importantly as far as my brother and I were concerned, established Hebrew schools, one of which Samuel and I attended.

We wore uniforms to school, little black suits with jackets that buttoned up to our collars. Every Passover our school would close for the full eight days and that's when we would get outfitted in a new suit.

As it turned out, Samuel was in the same class at our school as Dov Shilansky, who survived the Holocaust and emigrated to Israel in 1948. Upon arriving, he served as a combat officer in the Arab-Israeli war and later became speaker of the Israeli Knesset.

We strictly observed the holidays, and davened at shul on Friday evenings and Saturday morning. On Rosh Hashanah and Yom Kippur, you simply could not find a Jewish enterprise open for business.

Of course, as kids, we thought all Jews were like us. We didn't have the concept of Reform, Conservative or Orthodox.

Siauliai was a center of Zionist activities. To a great degree this was a response to the anti-semitism that had surrounded and oppressed Jews in Eastern Europe for centuries and was becoming palpable again after World War

I. Zionists wanted to re-establish the Jewish homeland in the historic Land of Israel, also known as Palestine.

This yearning for a separate and distinct homeland dates back millennia and my parents had it in their bones. The Jewish Diaspora, the scattering of our people across the globe, began in 586 BCE when the Babylonians destroyed the first Jewish Temple in the historic land of Israel. Since then Jews have almost always been in the minority wherever they lived and were often discriminated against and oppressed.

Zionism and the drive to re-create a homeland gained momentum in 19th century Europe in response to rampant anti-Semitism but also at a time when Jews had sufficient resources to begin to make things happen.

Some of you reading these recollections already know this history better than me. But I always like to add a historical footnote or two when I go out and speak to young people. Young Jews need to know where they came from so they can figure out where they are going to go.

And, of course, I talk to many young people who are not Jewish. They know a bit about the Holocaust, but have little idea about what came before or even much that came after. Nothing gives me greater pleasure than to hear what a young member of a minority community makes of our history. We have much in common and much that we can learn from one another.

Many Jewish families, including ours, set their sights on someday moving to Palestine. We were members of Betar, at the time a nascent nationalist group that encouraged Jews

On his grade-school photo, Mendel is in the first row at far right

to resettle in Palestine. We went to meetings, wore special uniforms and participated in drills, which, as it turned out, were not without purpose. Some Betar members would lead the Jewish resistance to Nazis in eastern Europe.

It wasn't a matter of if, just when for us to move to Palestine. My father – as many Jewish patriarchs did – purchased a plot of land in a village known as Yokneam. It was established for Jews in 1935 as a rural settlement camp and has come quite a long way since then. (Yokneam, not far from Haifa, is now known as Israel's "Startup Village," a high-tech hub.) The best time to make the move to Yokneam, my father figured, would be when we completed our high school studies in Siauliai. For me, the youngest, that would have been the summer of 1946.

So much would happen before then and almost none of it good.

***

These historic crosscurrents were unknown to me as a small child. I was focused mainly on having fun. We would wake up in the morning, have our breakfast, and ride our bikes to school. All classes were conducted in Hebrew, the better to prepare for the days when we would live in Palestine.

We also spoke Yiddish, which is a central/eastern European mix of Hebrew, German and Russian that evolved over many centuries. This is the language we spoke to each other at home. We spoke Lithuanish as well which has roots in both Slavic and Germanic languages. Then, of course, we also learned to speak German and Russian. This helped us to deal with everyone who would cross our path.

We did not mix very much with non-Jews, though we were certainly happy when they patronized our store. Histories from the period will document that Jews faced a great deal of animosity from non-Jewish Lithuanians. But I do not remember any incidents particular to my brother and me. We lived in a bit of a bubble.

Not all of our Jewish friends were particularly observant, but most were. We kept an Orthodox home. My family was charitable. My grandmother would give me challahs to deliver to the poor and pay me 50 cents to make the deliveries. I would use that 50 cents to attend movies in our neighborhood.

My parents employed a housekeeper, who would cook and care for us while they tended the store. In the spring, we spent our afternoons playing soccer and in the winter, residents flooded a tennis court where we could ice skate.

My favorite memories are probably from the summer. We would go to the seashore, most often to Palanga, a resort town (and it remains that to this day) on the Baltic Sea about 90 miles west of Siauliai. My father could not take the summer off from the store, so he would join us on weekends.

Palanga was quite the place back then. The president of LIthuania stayed there, along with other high government officials, and members of the intelligentsia, writers and artists. They could be seen walking the beaches, along the dunes and taking advantage of curative baths and imbibing on mineral water from artesian wells.

Not far away were pine forests where we would go hiking. In the evening you could find concerts and plays in the public parks.

I don't want to put too fine a point on this, but when you think about what was in store for us just a couple of years later, well it was simply more than an adolescent such as I was then could possibly comprehend. And even today, I struggle with how to keep it all in a proper perspective.

Now this is the only part of the book that it is x-rated. My father used to take us to a nude beach. There was one for men and another for women. But most of our days were spent at the beach for everyone with the conventional attire. I remember my mother waiting with a blanket for us to come

Mendel's brother, Samuel, stands tall behind his teacher

out of the water because even though it was summer, we were pretty far north and you could get quite a chill.

As mentioned, I was the youngest by a year and a half, and my brother didn't particularly enjoy having me tag along. I couldn't say we were rivals as he had his own interests and he was looking ahead of himself, not behind. We would have our scrapes, though mostly over nonsense like who would get the biggest portion at dinner.

Of course, to this point in our lives neither Samuel nor I knew the meaning of deprivation.

Those lessons began arriving at our doorstep in the summer of 1940, just a couple of months before my 12th birthday.

Simon and Recha Rosenberg with their
two young sons, Samuel, left, and Mendel

2

The Gathering Storm

I have only a vague recollection what happened and the feelings I had when my parents lost control of our fate. On one day Samuel and I were going to school and our parents were going to the store, and on another, our parents were put out of work and we were told we would be attending another school.

I can tell you why it happened. The Soviets and the Germans had arrived at a deal that carved our little section of the world into pieces they would control. The so-called Molotov-Ribbentrop Non-Aggression Pact in January 1939 called for the Germans to either annex or dominate territory to their east including Poland and for the Russians to have control over territory to the west, which included the Baltic states of Lithuania, Latvia and Estonia. Thus, the Russians and the Germans would keep the peace among themselves which in turn allowed Hitler to turn his country's military might against the British and the French. Britain and France declared war on the Germans in September of 1939 after German forces invaded Poland

The Soviet Union moved into Lithuania in June 1940 and actually annexed our country two months later. As bad as that was, it was worse for those living in German-occupied Poland. More than a quarter of a million Polish refugees came over the border to Lithuania to escape the Germans.

It's likely our parents who kept up with the news of the day had some understanding of what was in store for them and their fellow Lithuanians and that it would not be good. But I am certain they had no idea of the cruelty and barbarity that would result. Our lives went from merely bad to worse to unfathomably horrible. With each passing week we believed things couldn't get worse, though we kept hearing rumors about what was happening in the German-occupied sectors. Even if true, my parents thought, that couldn't happen where we were living and certainly not to us.

So let's begin with what was merely awful. The Soviets moved into our town and took the family store away from us. They were Communists and did not believe in private enterprise. The keys were handed over to a woman who had worked in our store and now would manage it. My parents were told not to return.

My father was nothing if not resourceful, and after some time he was able to land a construction job. My mother stayed home with us. But our home life was about to change as well. The Russians decided to bivouac their military personnel and their families in our apartment building. They took away

Mendel's maternal grandparents with other family

two of our rooms and put two Russian families in with us. Along with the crowding, we were dealing with families who had no understanding of our kosher kitchen. Thankfully, the Russians weren't looking to pick a fight with us. We got some electric hot plates and asked our co-tenants to cook their meals in their own rooms, which they did.

This sort of encroachment was happening all across the town, and, as far as we could tell, it had nothing to do with us being Jewish. The communists were atheists, and were hostile to all people of faith. All Lithuanians were living under their thumb and mostly we just tried to stay out of the way of our occupiers.

But sometimes we unwittingly got out of line. I can remember playing in the park with my friends and taking pictures with a box camera. Suddenly a soldier came over, grabbed my camera and took the film out ruining my photos. He said we should not take any pictures of them. I am pretty sure I hadn't aimed my camera at them, but it didn't matter.

We learned that the Soviets were capable of much worse than this. Soviet soldiers came for my aunt and uncle, Sonia and Issac Ehrlich, my cousins, Bluma and Khasya and deported them to Siberia. (See Chapter 3.)

As hard as it was for the Ehrlichs in the summer of 1941, it became even more difficult for us. I know my parents by this time wanted to leave for Palestine or the west. But by then it was impossible.

I don't remember the exact date, but as the history books tell us, it must have been around late June 1941 when we began to hear bombs falling near our town. The Germans were invading. Thankfully none of the bombs struck in our neighborhood, but more than 4,000 civilians across Lithuania died in the Luftwaffe's initial attacks.

Nevertheless, many Lithuanians welcomed the Germans as liberators. Some of our fellow citizens even participated in reprisals against the Jews as the Nazis claimed they sympathized with the Bolsheviks and should be eliminated.

This happened in stages. In that first year, 1941, many Jews were simply rounded up and murdered. Then in 1942, many were herded into ghettos surrounded by barbed wire. In the spring of 1943, the Germans emptied the ghettos, shot the oldest and the weakest and sent off the others to concentration camps.

Unlike other occasions where word of the roundups and shootings came to us as rumblings and rumors and happened to other people, the Holocaust came to our front door.

Mendel's mom, Recha, and her brother, Isaac
Ehrlich in a photo from the early 1900s.

3

Another Kind of Hell – Deportation

According to Holocaust histories, more than 17,000 Lithuanians citizens were taken to Siberia just before the Nazi invasion and many political prisoners were simply murdered. Among the deportees were my uncle and aunt, Isaac and Sonia Ehrlich, and their two daughters, Bluma, then 12 years old, and Khasya, nine.

Bluma, who is now living near me in St. Louis County, remembers vividly the day the Soviet soldiers came for her family. They showed up at 6 o'clock in the morning on June 14, 1941.

Here is Bluma's account:

"We were told we would be leaving in a short time and that we could take 100 kilograms of our belongings. I went out the back way as my parents prepared to depart we knew not where. My mission was to tell Mendel and

his family what was going on so they could prepare themselves as well. We had no sense of why we were being taken and not others. Only later did we come to believe that the Soviets, somewhat in a panic, wanted to make sure to remove any citizens who might support the Germans. That, of course, would never be us. But there was no way they could know that.

"They put us on a train meant to transport animals not humans. And for three days it didn't move.

"When the train finally rolled out, we were in for a journey that would cover 3,000 miles (about the same distance as from Seattle to New York) and take two weeks. There were about 30 people packed into our car, and we had a hole in the floor where we could defecate. The car was equipped with planks where we could at least lie down.

"We were given rations once a day, usually some kind of soup, meat and bread.The provisions actually were reasonably generous, but in keeping with my faith I would not eat the pork that they provided."

The conditions in the area where the Ehrlichs ended up -- Tenyga, a village in the Siberian wilderness near the Mongolian border -- were brutal. Food and other provisions were scarce. Conditions improved marginally over the next two years when they were able to relocate to a large town, Gorno-Altaysk, 120 miles to the north. Both parents were able to land jobs, which entitled them to rations -- but only for themselves, not their children.

Sonia and Isaac Ehrlich

Bottom from left: Samuel; Simon, Mendel and Samuel's father; cousin Bluma; her father, Isaac Ehrlich; Mendel. Top: Recha, Mendel and Samuel's mother; Sonia, Bluma's mother

And so it was in 1943 that Bluma and Khasya's father died from what was essentially malnutrition. He had been giving his rations to his children. Isaac Ehrlich was just 49 years old.

Now widowed, Sonia managed to eke out a living as a cook and a seamstress. Before the war ended, Sonia, Khasya and Bluma moved to Biysk, an even larger city. The two sisters would go on to meet their husbands there. Bluma earned an associate's degree in medicine and became a nurse-practitioner and paramedic. Khasya became a math teacher, and she was considered one of the best in the region.

Conditions improved enough in the post-war years that Bluma's, daughter, Rekha, born in 1957, had more opportunities. She studied at a music conservatory in Krasnoyarsk, an industrial center and one of Siberia's largest cities. Her cousin, Fanya, Khasya's daughter, became an English language teacher. They found good men to marry and started households of their own. But as Jews in the Soviet Union, they recognized there would always be a limit on how far they could advance in their chosen careers.

Decades later, in the mid-to-late 1990s, Bluma, Khasya, their husbands, daughters and sons-in-law were allowed to emigrate to the U.S. as refugees. I along with other relatives living in the United States were in the fortunate position of acting as their sponsors.

Top: Bluma. Bottom from left, Samuel, grandma Sora Ehrlich, Khasya, and Mendel.

Mendel's mother and father, Recha and Simon Rosenberg

Jewish leaders rounded up before being shot, including
Mendel's dad, third prisoner from left

4

Bad to Worse for the Rosenbergs

The Germans made quick work of the Soviet forces in the Baltics and came marching into our town in late June 1941. One of the first things they did was round up all the Jews and they had plenty of help from the non-Jewish residents.

As I mentioned, the Germans, at least to some degree, were seen as liberators. Hardly anyone liked the Russians. So my fellow non-Jewish citizens were of a mind to be helpful. Without them, the Germans wouldn't know who was Jewish and who wasn't. Once they learned who was who, the Germans took many of the men and teenagers to jail. My father and my brother, then 15, were among those in the first wave of arrests. The soldiers armed with rifles showed up at our door and took them away. Simple as that.

Somehow we learned from others that the Germans were accepting bribes and that we might be able to rescue my father and brother if we showed up with some money. My brother was freed on a Sunday, but it was too late for my father. On the previous Friday, he had been separated from my brother. On Saturday, he along with some other men were taken outside of town and told to dig a huge ditch, which would become their grave. My father and dozens of other men were gunned down at the site. My brother learned of this while still in jail. I do not know how the word got back to him.

I have a picture of my father that was taken just before his execution. It came to me many years later from a friend who had run away with the Russians. That friend, Zelig Gilinski, returned to Lithuania after the war and was able go through some files and find the photograph. The Germans, as is well known, were meticulous record keepers and there are many photos documenting the atrocities they committed. Based on those records Holocaust historians have estimated that the Germans and Lithuanian nationals murdered about a thousand Jews during the first two weeks of the occupation.

We were, of course, much relieved to bring Samuel back into our home. But learning of my father's death was a heavy blow. We were so unprepared for something like that. It took me a long time to comprehend that my father was never going to return. I tried to persuade myself that, no, this isn't real. He will be coming back.

We sat shiva for father, but really there was no time for grieving. Soon, new tenants were moving into our home. These were Lithuanians who had come to the city from the

Stone marking site of Trakai Street ghetto in Siauliai

suburbs. Their homes had been destroyed in the fight. We were now living with three sisters who were put in one of our bedrooms.

If you can find any humor in our plight, this was the occasion. The sisters began entertaining German soldiers in their bedroom. As word got around, the soldiers would gather at our door and wait their turn. We lived on the second story and they stood in a line that snaked down the steps all the way to the street. At one point the soldiers became interested in my grandmother, but thankfully they did her no harm.

This situation did not last long as the Germans had something even worse in store for us. In July of 1941, they identified two neighborhoods they would establish as ghettos for all Jewish residents. They erected barbed-wire fencing around the neighborhoods, and forced us out of our homes. We only could take what we would carry. (After we left, many Lithuanians went into our homes and took what remained, making a lot of money by selling our possessions.)

When all was said and done the Germans pushed an estimated 5,000 Jews into the buildings within the ghettos. There was the Kaukaza ghetto, with about 200 houses in poor condition, and the Trakai ghetto, with about 110 houses, which is where we were forced to live. They were named after the streets where they were situated, about a quarter of a mile apart.

The area was quite small for so many people, just about two acres. How large is two acres? Think of the zoo in Forest Park, which covers 90 acres. The living area for 5,000 Jews was just twice the size of flight cage at the zoo. You could say the birds had it much better.

Those who were forced into the ghetto were actually fortunate in a way. When the crowding created more chaos than the Germans could handle, they considered creating a third ghetto. But perhaps they thought that was more trouble than it was worth. Instead, they began taking Jews in groups of 200 to 300 at a time to the Lieponiai forest and shot them.

As of Sept. 1, we were sealed into the ghettos. Lithuanian guards were posted at the gates. To get in and out, required a special permit. We were also made to wear yellow stars on the front and back of our clothing. Some of our fellow Jews resisted wearing those stars, but when they were found out, they would be beaten and jailed.

Most of us simply submitted to whatever we were told to do. We had had it so good for so long in Lithuania, we simply were unprepared for this kind of treatment and it seemed futile to resist.

Our living space amounted to a kitchen and one other room. My mother, grandmother, brother and I also shared our quarters with a woman and her son and daughter. My brother and I built bunks and we slept in the kitchen with the other woman's son. My mother and grandmother shared a bed. The other woman and her daughter slept in another.

Our days were spent on work details. I started working for a cabinetmaker. Little did I know that learning these skills would play a role in saving my life and also prepare me for the business I would start in the U.S. Along with the carpentry, Samuel and I worked in a sugar factory turning beets into sugar products.

We also worked in the rail yard, which, of course, was essential to the Germans who were moving troops back and forth. Later those trains would be used to take Jews from the ghettos to the concentration camps.

My mother was also sent out on work details to a shoe factory. Only my grandmother, too infirm to work, would stay behind. She would die of a heart attack within months, which while sad for all of us, turned out to be a blessing.

Well, you might wonder, how could that be. It wasn't long after her death that the Germans decided they wanted to rid themselves of any Jew who could not in some way be useful to them, infants, toddlers, and children up to about age six, the elderly and those with disabilities.

These separations were excruciating, especially when it involved the children. The Germans tried to make it seem as if the separations were temporary, saying that the children were going to be taken to a camp where they could get the appropriate care. By this time, most families were under no illusion about what was happening.

Obviously, there isn't one mother or father who would want to send away their children. But the Germans were not

Gates to the ghetto in Siauliai

to be denied. Anyone who interfered would be shot immediately. The Germans would get impatient and separate 20 people from those assembled. They would threaten to shoot that group and another every five minutes unless and until the families gave up their children. I remember in particular a Jewish resident who was delegated by the Germans to be in charge and assist them as needed. He tore his own child away from his wife and put the toddler on a truck as a means of setting an example for the others.

The separations created a chaotic scene with parents and children wailing, others whimpering, many saying the Kaddish, a mourning ritual prayer.

Then the next day, as if nothing much had happened, we all went out again on our work details. When my mother went out to her job she somehow was able to make contact with some non-Jewish Lithuanians who would give her some food that she could smuggle into the ghetto. For example she would wrap a napkin around an egg and put it in a kerchief that she would tie around her neck. Her long hair would hide the bulge in the kerchief. The food would not come free. She had to trade what was left of our belongings.

Meanwhile my brother and I would steal what items we could. For example, in the fall, we would be taken to farms to help with the harvest of sugar beets. While there, sympathetic farmers would provide us with things to eat. Later, at the factories we would make off with some product as well. Likewise, when we worked at the rail yards, we would fill our pockets with what we could find on the railcars.

We would also beg from the Germans who would sometimes pitch us a half-smoked cigarette. We then would trade the cigarettes for food. Here too is where my carpentry skills came in handy. I could fix things for the Germans who, though they didn't have to, would repay me with a few cigarettes.

As you may have guessed, there were Germans and then there were Germans. We tried to stay away from the guards and the SS. They would beat you with the butt of a rifle before they even answered a question. But there were members of the Wehrmacht, the regular German military, and some civilians as well, who could be decent.

At this point, we were not so afraid of getting shot as simply starving. The rations we were given were so small and you had to wait in line for hours to get them.

At times, one of us would fall ill and we were allowed to stay home. There were some Jewish doctors in the ghetto and they would attend to us. We suffered often from dysentery, but we learned how to take care of that ourselves. We found that burning a potato and eating the charred remains could help put an end to it.

Whatever was wrong, you couldn't stay sick for long because they would come and try to send you to a hospital. At least that is what they would tell you. Most people never returned from those so-called hospital visits.

Life was so irregular and upside down. I was 13 when the Germans sent us into the ghetto. Needless to say I would not be celebrating my Bar Mitzvah, as Samuel had two years earlier. That would come more than 50 years later, here in St. Louis.

We did try to maintain our holiday observances though we were forced to work during Shabbat. We prayed in the morning and in the evening as we could. During that time, my elders in the ghetto created some clandestine cultural and educational organizations to keep alive the dream of moving someday to Palestine. But we did not attend school.

In June of 1943, Heinrich Himmler called on the SS to liquidate the ghettos across Eastern Europe and move all Jews into concentration camps. In November, SS troops transported more than 800 children and elderly to Auschwitz. In July 1944, the Germans, by then retreating from the advancing Russians, transferred the remaining ghetto residents to concentration camps at Stutthof and Dachau.

Stutthof was very close to what is now Gdansk, Poland, about 250 miles southwest of Siauliai. Dachau was more than 900 miles away in southern Germany. Mother, Samuel and I were first sent to Stutthof where we stayed for a few months, then Samuel and I were put on a train to Dachau, a 700-mile journey. Mother would never see Samuel again. And it would be more than two years before mother and I were reunited.

Entrance to Stutthof concentration camp

5

A Family Torn Asunder

Mother, Samuel and I learned that we would be leaving the ghetto in perhaps the most impersonal way possible. A truck came down our street ordering us and our neighbors to come out of our buildings. There we found a line of cargo trucks that we were to board for a destination unknown.

We were allowed no possessions except the clothes we were wearing and whatever we could carry in our hands. We would not have any of it for very long.

The caravan took us to a rail yard where we boarded cattle cars that took us 250 miles south and west to Stutthof, a camp located near what is now Gdansk, Poland. For purposes of comparison, that is approximately the distance from St. Louis to Kansas City.

I am sure we wondered if our circumstances would get better or worse. In the ghetto we had heard rumors of atrocities. It didn't take long after our arrival to get the answer.

Stutthof sat in a fir and pine forest on the Baltic Coast in what once was and now is a beautiful setting. It had been the site of a home for the elderly, situated in a large house near a glade. In 1939, the SS arrived with a dozen prisoners and began to build a camp on 10 acres that in years to come would grow to 300 acres and hold more than 52,000 prisoners. In the first couple of years, it housed Polish political prisoners, who were used as forced laborers, then came Russians, gypsies, many other nationalities and, of course, Lithuanians like us. It was the first camp to be established in Poland and the last to be closed.

Triple-level bunks as preserved today at Stutthof camp

When we arrived, we were stood up in rows outside the camp and then they walked us in line by line.

I do not remember this specifically, but according to one Holocaust history (found at HolocaustResearchProject.org), new inmates received this greeting: "From now on you are no longer a person, just a number. All your rights have been left outside the gate – you are left with only one and that you are free to do – leave through that chimney." By that he meant the crematorium where they disposed of murdered inmates.

The guards separated the men and the women, then took us into a room and stripped us naked. They shaved all the hair from our bodies head to toe and subjected us to body cavity searches, looking for our valuables. We then were told to put on blue and white uniforms, our clothing for the duration of our captivity. We were also given a dish for the meager rations we would be getting.

We were shuttled into a barracks for about 70 to 100 people, men and women both, where we lived for several days as the Germans sorted through who was who and where we might be assigned for work duty.

Later we were assigned to barracks with three-story bunks. Ours had a washroom, lavatory and sleeping quarters. We slept on paper mattresses filled with wood shavings.

I suppose we were the lucky ones. Many arrived at the camp with a death warrant attached. Some were kept in windowless cells and were executed with a shooting before day's end. Others were taken to the crematorium where they were shot in the back of the head or hanged.

If the Germans didn't kill you, illness or disease could also take your life. Typhus and tuberculosis epidemics regularly broke out in the camp in 1944. The camp had a hospital, but if you were considered incurable, you were not going to get treatment. If the disease did not take you quickly, the Germans might inject you with phenol, a toxic carbolic acid compound, or drown you in a bath, according to the Holocaust Research Project history. The killings and the deaths from disease were so numerous that it overwhelmed the crematorium. So the Germans set up a pyre in which piles of bodies were placed on a row of logs, then topped with more logs, then more bodies and so forth. Then it all would be doused with fuel oil and set aflame.

Samuel and I were at Stutthof just a month or so and were not assigned to work details, which was fortunate. Some prisoners were taken outside the camp to work 12-hour shifts and others performed work at the camp. The prisoners might be assigned to clear land, dig sewers and trenches or build roads.

They were doing this work while subsisting on about 1,000 calories a day. That's essentially a couple of bowls of soup made with scraps of cabbage, turnips or carrots and a hunk of dark bread perhaps with some margarine or jam.

Public hangings were common. They were a means of imposing discipline and Samuel and I and the others were forced to watch as other inmates took their punishment. We were never given a reason for the hangings. Somehow this made our memory of the ghetto less brutal. There you were

Guard tower at Stutthof concentration camp

told what to do and if you didn't do it, the punishment was not so swift. When and if it came, they took you out of the ghetto and shot you. Here in the camp it took place for all to witness.

As mentioned, our stay would not be long at Stutthof as the Germans were in need of workers in the heartland of their own country. Also the Russians were closing in – they had turned the tide against the Germans in the battle for Stalingrad, in the winter of 1943 and were marching to the west. (They would arrive at Stutthof in early 1945, about six months after we departed.)

By the time we left, we had been separated from our mother for a few weeks. We did not have a chance to see her and say goodbye before we were taken away in trucks and again loaded into a cattle car with about 70 other men. In all, about 3,000 inmates were transported on the day we departed.

It is just 750 miles to Dachau as the crow flies, but our route was not so direct and it took days as the train would pull over to sidings for hours at a time, which we assumed was to allow higher priority trains to get through.

We were so crowded on those cattle cars that men had to sit with other men between their legs and you had to sleep sitting upright. There were no bathroom facilities, just a bucket to relieve yourself, which was emptied just once a day when the train stopped, and when we were given our one meal for the day.

Believe it or not, it was a relief to get to our next concentration camp. Some of the men never made it off the train, they died en route or were too weak to disembark.

But Samuel and I survived the trip in reasonably good shape. As the guards began lining everyone up I noticed they were separating us into age groups. I was keen on staying with my older brother, as we had never been separated whether it was under the Soviets, in the Siauliai ghetto or at Stutthof.

So when the guards looked the other way, I ran to be with Samuel in a group of older youths, and raised myself on my tiptoes to look as old as they were.

It worked.

All of us prisoners got off at Dachau where Samuel and I were to stay only a few days. We were then shipped out to a sub-camp at Muhldorf, about 70 miles away. As bad as all of this had been, our next six months would be the worst. I had just turned 16. Samuel was 17 and would not see 18.

The gate to the Dachau camp says "Work sets you free"

6

Life and Death at Dachau

At Muhldorf, you could say the Germans added insult to injury. Not only were we subjected to starvation and privation of all sorts, we were helping with their war effort. The Dachau concentration camp was among Germany's first, located on the site of a former World War I munitions factory, just 20 miles from Munich.

Heinrich Himmler opened the camp in 1933, not long after Hitler took power and used it as a site to imprison Communists. Along with the prison, the Nazis used the site to train SS officers, who quickly became notorious for terrorizing Jews across Germany. The Jewish population at the camp grew after 1935 and increased markedly after Kristallnacht in November 1938, when the Germans essentially conducted a riot against the Jews and took them from their homes. A few years later as the Nazis began the systematic slaughter of the Jewish population, they began transferring the Dachau inmates to mass extermination camps in Poland.

In the summer of 1944 and with the Allied forces closing in from the west and the Russians from the east, the Germans created 36 sub camps near armament facilities around Dachau to support the war effort. Muhldorf was one of those sites.

When Samuel and I arrived at Muhldorf we found a new facility with fresh barbed wire and electrified fences. Again we found bunks stacked in threes with mattresses made of straw. Our daily ration was half a loaf of bread with soup in the morning, noon and in the evening.

These were not hearty soups like you see on Campbell's commercials. Our soup was made of grass, perhaps a bit of celery and on a good day some potatoes. We carried our utensils with us and put them aside when we went to work.

Memorial to Muhldorf camp victims

We all had been conscripted into Organization Todt, a manufacturer supporting the German war effort. Many Germans who could not serve in the military were forced into some kind of auxiliary service and working for OT, as it was called, was one option. Also working at the various OT facilities were prisoners of war, and anyone else the Germans could get their hands on to help in those final desperate months as they tried to turn back the Allied forces.

One of our jobs was to make concrete for bunkers and the like. Many of our days were spent hauling sand to the cement mixers, a backbreaking task. We would start in the morning with a three-mile walk to the construction site, a trip that in itself became more and more difficult with each passing day as our strength began to ebb.

When we arrived we'd make cement and carry sand to different areas. At times we mixed the cement and carried it to spots where other workers built bunkers and housing. After several months working around the cement, I was completely wasted, in part because I suffered from dysentery and couldn't hold what little nourishment I got. Unlike in the past, we could not sneak away to forage for food.

I was unable to stop working to relieve myself. I had to wait till I got back to the barracks to clean up. This was not an easy task in the winter as the water was freezing. Even when not battling dysentery, my clothing was almost always infested with lice, as were those of the others.

We did have a couple of stoves in the barracks. We would boil water and use it to kill off the lice and wash our clothing as best we could. We would then put our clothing inside the stove in such a way as to dry it without burning it up.

I believe I went more than two years without ever bathing in warm water.

People have asked me whether we prayed, or somehow kept the Sabbath. For the most part, we were simply trying to survive and every day one or more of us would simply give up, lie down or fall and wait for a bullet or the butt of a rifle to end our lives.

But yes, I do remember makeshift Rosh Hashanah and Yom Kippur services in the fall of 1944 before our work shift. I am uncertain if we had our services on the right day. Perhaps someone was keeping track, but we had no calendar to keep and had only the rising and the setting of the sun to mark the beginning and the end of our days. Of course, we had no prayer books, nor Tallits (prayer shawls), and no Torah. Some of the older people who knew most everything by heart started off and the rest of us followed along as best we could.

You could say this was our form of resistance, of our continuing identification with our faith, of our solidarity with one another. In hindsight it certainly was, but really at the time, each one of us was just trying to make it to another day. We were fighting hopelessness more than we were our captors.

One thing that provided just a bit of cheer was the rumors we were hearing from the *kapos*. The *kapos* were the prisoners among us who made sure we followed the rules and they reported to the Germans. They would hear that things were not going well on both the eastern and western fronts. We would also hear from the German work details that sometimes worked alongside of us.

At this stage of the war, the German civilians were enduring privations that while not nearly as severe as our own, were difficult. They didn't have a lot of food, or cigarettes, or much of anything. Even so, a few of them might share a morsel or two of food with us by giving us their container to wash for them and leaving a little bit inside.

As fall turned into winter, our situation became far worse. In our sub camp, hundreds were perishing each day. The overall population did not diminish as the Germans were bringing in more prisoners, particularly from Hungary as I recall. They and the others were called "fresh meat," as in a fresh supply for the work force.

News of new arrivals and our various work situations made up most of the discussion in the barracks. We would also talk about what we could possibly do to stay warm. We learned from each other to take the cement sacks from work and cut holes in them and wear them as outer clothing. We would take the paper from the cement bags and wrap them around our feet, as we had been given no socks.

In early 1945, I was simply running out of energy. I was getting sick too often and at age 16 I felt like I had one foot in the grave. Of course, I would never ask for medical help. The camp had a hospital, but we knew from rumor and our own observations that the doctors were using us for experiments. We would see the twisted bodies of their victims outside the facilities.

On the work details, the guards were brutal toward anyone who faltered. If a prisoner died either from exhaustion or the blows that he took from a guard, he was loaded on a truck that followed along just for the purpose of transporting bodies. There was an accounting at the beginning and end of each day of who had died and we all had to wait in formation as this was done. The Germans were meticulous about keeping track.

Then came a bit of good fortune. There happened to be some people at Muhldorf who had known my parents. They had jobs working inside the camp carpenter shop. When they saw me, they told the *kapos* they were short handed and needed more help. You will remember that when I was in the ghetto I was given a job where I learned carpentry. So I had some skills to offer.

When working in the carpenter shop, I did not have to face the elements and walk to construction sites. We were assigned all kind of work inside the camp from fixing the barracks to constructing tables and chairs.

Also while we were working in the carpenter shop, we had an opportunity to walk around freely in the camp with a toolbox. We used our carpentry skills to build false bottoms in the tool box to hide whatever we could lay our hands on, such as food that had been tossed in the garbage.

But Samuel was not so fortunate. Around the time I got into the carpenter shop, Samuel got transferred to another sub camp where the inmates lived in tents. January and February 1945 were among the coldest winter months of the

20th century in Europe, with blizzards and temperatures well below zero.

One day Samuel left for his work detail and never came back. I tried looking to find out where he was. I asked if I could be transferred to where he was. But I was refused.

After the war I found out that sometime in February, Samuel had been beaten to death by one of the *kapos*. I do not know what Samuel might have done to draw the attention of the *kapo*. At that point, you could get killed for almost anything.

A recent winter day at what's left of Dachau

I was still simply trying to survive, and this made that task all the more difficult. I had lost my tie to the last person close to me. My papa and grandmother had perished. For all I knew my mother was dead, too. And now my brother had gone missing.

Flowers adorn a railcar that once transported Nazi victims

Still, I held on to hope. The German civilians were telling us the war seemed to be coming to an end and not in a good way for them. They said their high command had been inducting a lot of old men and children to stave off the

Russians who were coming very close to their pre-war borders. The Americans were already in Germany proper.

Then in late April, all the able-bodied prisoners – thousands at that time – were ordered on to rail cars. It was another rail journey in many ways like the others that came before. But this time we all had the feeling that an end was coming to all of this. Only this journey was much longer – 10 days. We got very little food, hardly any water, and our train came to a stop many times before we learned what would ultimately be in store for us.

Nearly starved survivors of a Nazi camp

7

Liberation

As our train headed down the tracks to an unknown destination, we wondered what would happen to us. Holocaust historians would learn that the Germans wanted to take us into the Tyrolian Alps where SS troops would dispose of us in a place where the advancing American troops would be unlikely to find us. The Germans, knowing they faced certain defeat, would not want to leave any evidence that would lead to reprisals against them.

Again, I found myself packed into a cattle car with 70 people, with no food and no way to stay clean. The stench was overwhelming. We got some water by collecting rainwater from the roof of the car. I would later learn that there were dozens of boxcars like ours with 3,000 captives.

At one point our train came to a halt. And the most curious among us began to peer out the window. Then we stepped out to find that the guards had run off.

We thought at last we were free, but we had the misfortune of being near an air field where there were soldiers.

When they saw what was going on, they starting shooting at those who were furthest from the train. I took two bullets in my leg. Many of the guards returned and forced us back into the rail cars.

The train's fits and starts had us confused. What we learned later is that some Germans did not want to see us massacred. According to one historical account, a Wehrmacht transport commander kept delaying the train so it could be liberated by the advance units of the US Army.

The journey continued – I think we are on the train for a total of 10 days – until the morning of May 5. The train had stopped and we could hear nothing outside the door. One of the captives peered out through an opening and seeing no one around clambered out. Then he came around to open the door. Some of the captives got off and began running. A few shouted, "There are the Americans right down the highway." And it was true, There they were with trucks and jeeps. And we were so happy. We finally made it. We beat the odds. We were alive. Survivors.

But barely.

We had so little strength. At first the Americans shared canned goods with us, but we had no way to open them. I finally got a can open by smashing it on a rock. I found meat inside, the first meat I'd had in four years.

For a while it was catch as catch can with the provisions, but it wasn't long before the Red Cross came to us and set up kitchens where they fed us from early in the morning to late at night.

The Americans and the United Nations Relief Agency had a huge task dealing with all the survivors they found just at this site, not to mention all those found in camps across Europe. They set up a refugee center in Feldafing, just 30 miles from Dachau, which would be home for me and thousands of others. I lived there for two years -- some stayed longer -- until we could find a place to go, to restart our lives.

I was then just 16. In the previous three years, I had lost my grandmother, my father, and my brother, and had been separated from my mother. But soon I would be able to stitch my life back together again. Somehow a line of communication was established among the various refugee centers. My mother who had remained in the Stutthof camp till the end of the war got word to me that I should stay put. She would come to me and then we would figure out what to do and where we should go.

Of course, she would need money to do this, and this is where we had some good fortune. After her release from Stutthof, mother was able to return to Siauliai to the neighborhood near the ghetto where we had stayed. One day in 1944, while on a work detail, she was able to bury a bit of gold in the garden of a friend. After all this time, she dug into the garden and found the gold was still there. She was able to use it to convert it into currency that allowed her to both pay and bribe her way through a variety of agencies so she could gain access to Feldafing.

But it wasn't until July or August of 1946 that she arrived. By then I had spent more than a year in Feldafing as a stateless youth, living in a UN compound with 4,000 other refugees, attending a makeshift school and working as a carpenter. You hear much about refugee centers these days, many of which only address basic needs and are meant to be short lived. The refugee camp at Feldafing would remain open eight years until 1953.

As you might imagine, with a population of highly educated Jews, a society of sorts developed at Feldafing. The compound had newspapers, a library, schools – secular, religious, and vocational – theater and an orchestra. This was heaven compared to where I had been, but I was living with so much uncertainty as were all the others. Many of those around me were hoping to emigrate to Israel. In October 1945, David Ben-Gurion, then the de facto leader of the Jewish community in Palestine, and soon to become Israel's first prime minister, visited Feldafing. That gave many of the camp's residents a sense of possibility and hope that they could settle in Palestine.

When mother arrived, it was quite a shock and surprise. I knew she was coming, but had no idea when. I was working at the time in the carpenter shop when some people came running to me telling me that I had company. We fell into each others arms and wept with joy.

She had come to me with only the clothes on her back, and the money she had been able to save from her stash of gold. I had very little as well. But I had saved for her the treats from the Red Cross packages we received on a regular basis and from the compensation we got for working in the camp.

I loved seeing my mother again, but she looked different. Her time at Stutthof had aged her considerably and her hair, once raven colored, had gone completely gray. I must have looked different to her as well. I left her at age 14 in 1944 with

Mendel (right) at a carpentry workshop at the Feldafing refugee center

my head shaved to the nub, and now was nearly 17 with a full head of wavy hair.

We would stay at Feldafing several more months, which was made easier because we were given a whole room to ourselves in one of the large two-story buildings that provided shelter for the refugees. There we could set up housekeeping and be a family again. And, of course, even though I had grown up quite a bit, and had been fending for myself for two years, our relationship returned to normal. It was Mendel, do this. Mendel do that, along with lots of advice I didn't want to hear. I was still her boy.

Unlike many of the others at Feldafing, we did not see a future for ourselves in Palestine. Though my father had invested in some land, we had no family there, no one to take us in and help us get started.

But we did have cousins in the United States, Isaac and Ruth Bernstein in Youngstown, Ohio. So we wrote to them, and hoped they would respond, which most fortunately they did. In all, it took six months to get the paperwork done and get our tickets ready.

We boarded a train in Munich – a passenger train this time – and traveled to Hamburg where we had booked passage on a ship bound for the the land of the free and the home of the brave.

But it was March and that, we learned, is one of the worst times to set sail. Many passengers got quite seasick, including mother and me. I spent most of my time on a deck chair covered with a blanket in a small alcove. I would bring food down to my mother, but she was so sick she couldn't eat. Our voyage took two weeks and it was pretty horrible, even for a couple of people who had survived concentration camps. But we knew we were going to a better place and we just counted the days until we would get there.

During that time, we met and talked with others Holocaust survivors. We saw people we had known in Lithuania. But there were others from all over Europe speaking a dozen different languages. We could communicate with many of them because we could speak several languages. My mother knew German, French, Russian, and, of course, Yiddish. I knew German, Russian and Yiddish as well.

But there was one language with which we were barely acquainted: English. I listened intently to the English speakers so I could get a running start when we arrived in America.

And, finally, there came the day when the New York skyline came into view and, of course, the Statue of Liberty, just like you see in so many movies.

Our cousin was there to meet us. He showed us around New York for a couple of days and took us to the Empire State Building. I remember thinking it was so immense, I could hardly believe they could construct a building so tall without it simply toppling over.

Then it was off to Youngstown to begin life anew. By then our resources were depleted. My mother and I each carried $10 in our pockets. But we were brimming with hope.

8

Living the American Dream

When we arrived in Youngstown, Ohio, we found ourselves in what might be called the middle of somewhere. Youngstown is almost exactly between Cleveland to the northwest and Pittsburgh to the southeast. About 60-65 miles each way. And it's also almost exactly in the middle between New York to the east and Chicago to the west. About 400 miles either way.

Youngstown is in a region that is now known as the rust belt, having at one point been a center for steel manufacturing and coal mining. The community has lost more than 60 percent of its population from a near peak of 168,000 when I was living there to just 64,000 today.

But when I arrived with my mother in 1949, Youngstown was bustling, and with a substantial Jewish community that supported four congregations. The Bernsteins were members of the oldest and largest congregation Rodef Shalom, a reform synagogue, founded in 1867. Though not yet entirely accepted by the elite, Jews in Youngstown at mid-century were very much part of the merchant class. Many started with small retail businesses – at least 100 were grocers, including the man who would become my father-in-law, Gus Cohen.

Mendel and his mother in Youngstown, Ohio, 1953

Quite a few moved into more substantial enterprises. I was lucky enough to find work with one of the up and comers – the Friedken family, who lived in the same neighborhood as the Bernsteins, and who had just established Benada Aluminum (named for Ben Friedken, and his wife, Ada). The company over the years established extrusion operations in Ohio and Pennsylvania and window assembly facilities in Youngstown, St. Louis, Chicago, Minneapolis, Philadelphia, Baltimore and New York.

At the time I came on the scene, the Friedkens were looking for workers to build their windows. Introductions were made and I mentioned to Ben in my halting English that I had learned carpentry in Lithuania. He hired me to make storm windows at his plant, starting at 85 cents an hour. I would work for Benada for 20 years. And while I had my ups and downs with the company, it led to my meeting and marrying my wonderful wife, Sandy, who was Ben and Ada's niece. She did the bookkeeping in the front office. The knowledge I gained and the contacts I made through Benada helped me establish my own storm window business in St. Louis.

Cousin Isaac Bermstien amd wife Ruth

But more about that later. I had to learn English and I needed to finish my education, which I did by going to night school. That made for long days as I was working a 9-5 dayshift at Benada about five miles down the road in the town of Girard. Then I'd grab a bite to eat and take adult classes from 6-10 p.m. four nights a week in Youngstown. I needed 26 credits and finally got them after a few years. (An amusing sidebar: When I got to St. Louis in the 1960s, I wanted to get the actual diploma and sent away for it. It was only then that I learned that I was still short an American history credit. I studied up and took and passed my American history exam. I finally got my diploma when I was in my early thirties.)

I was driven. I wanted to recover everything that my family had before the war. All of it. To get it, I knew I had to learn English, get an education, get a good job and make money. 1-2-3-4, just like that.

And then there was No. 5. Have a family. When I met Sandy Cohen, I courted her avidly. Sandy's parents took a shine to me. Gus and Ruth noted that I was nine years older

Youngstown Vindicator

Ohio

Sandra Cohen Wed at Temple

Married under a floral canopy were Miss Sandra Cohen, daughter of Mr. and Mrs. Gus Cohen, 515 Willis Ave. and Mendel Rosenberg, son of the late Mrs. Recha Rosenberg, the ceremony taking place at Temple Emanu-El on Saturday, Dec. 28, at 6:30 p.m.

The bride wore a full length gown of mira-mist taffeta, having a flattering portrait neckline enhanced by hand-clipped lace glistening with tiny seed pearls and crystal sequins. Shirred sides of the midriff met the full bouffant skirt having appliques of lace on the sides, and the back had a butterfly bustle and sweeping chapel train. Her silk illusion veil was attached to a Queen

Mendel and Sandy met in Youngstown after the war and wed in 1957

than Sandy and advised her not to trifle with my affections. They knew my courtship was meant to lead to something.

Sandy knew where I came from and what I had been through, but I did not share my ghetto and concentration camp experiences with her in great detail. I did not mention it at all to anyone who I met in school or at work. I wanted very much to put it behind me.

But that was not so easy.

I had nightmares of being chased, shot at, and beaten. In one nightmare, with Nazis in pursuit, I entered an outhouse and jumped into the toilet. Sandy would hear me cry out in the night. Years later my children, Stuart and Renee, would hear it as well. Sandy told them not to ask me about it.

When you have a nightmare like this, you are so happy when you wake up and find you are safe and sound in America. These days, people would advise you to get some counseling or some kind of help. They might even call it Post Traumatic Stress Disorder. In those days, few would consider getting that kind of help.

Even with all of that, I could say my life was moving along splendidly. I was getting raises and promotions at work, and thinking about becoming a U.S. citizen. But even before that could take place, Uncle Sam wanted me. In January 1951, the Selective Service called on me to report to Fort Knox, Ky. to help out in the Korean War effort.

Given that I wasn't yet a citizen, I possibly could have opted out of the draft. But I very much wanted to serve the nation that had come to my rescue just six years before.

I filled out my induction papers noting that I could speak Russian and German fluently and maybe partly as a result, the Army sent me to military intelligence school at Ft. Meade. I figured I would be shipped to Europe.

Instead I was transferred to Pennsylvania as an MP guarding a stockade for American soldiers. This was not a good fit for me. I was instructed that if a prisoner was running away, I should shoot him. Well, you could imagine with the experience I had as a captive, I could not shoot a non-combatant, and certainly not an American, whose country saved me from the Nazis. I sought and was given a transfer within two weeks. I was made a company clerk.

In 1952, it came time for me to go overseas. I asked for a posting in Europe, hoping to provide some benefit to the

Mendel in Tokyo

Armed Forces with my language skills. And naturally the Army saw fit to send me to …. Japan.

I was assigned to a division involved in fixing half-tracks and tanks. Japanese workers did the actual work and the Americans provided the supervision. My job was to keep track of the inventory – the parts and tools. That experience was helpful when I later started my own business.

I returned to the states and received my discharge papers in December of 1952. Because of my service, I was able to become a naturalized citizen very quickly the following year.

Returning to Benada, and with some management experience under my belt, I asked to move from the factory floor to the front office. Permission granted.

The year 1957 was when everything changed for me. In April, I came home after an evening out with Sandy to find my cousin, Yitzok, waiting for me in the living room of the apartment I had been sharing with my mother. Having no way to reach me while I was out with Sandy, he had waited for me to deliver some very bad news. Mother had suffered a massive and fatal heart attack.

Mother had enjoyed the last few years, teaching Hebrew at Rodef Shalom and watching me rise through the ranks at Benada. But she was gone too soon. I am certain the trauma and stress she endured in losing her husband and eldest child during the war and her time in the ghetto and at the Stutthof camp took many years off her life. She died at age 62.

Not long after, my supervisors gave me another opportunity, a chance to take over management of their new plant in St. Louis. I was eager to make the move, but as previously noted, I had my eye on that beautiful woman keeping the books at Benada. It was time to pop the question and Sandy made me the happiest man in the world when she said yes. We married in December 1957 (…and still are together. We celebrated our 60th anniversary in 2017.)

I ran St. Louis operations for Benada until 1967, exactly 10 years – and 20 years overall with the company. At that point, I got some very bad news, especially for a guy with a wife and two small children. Benada dismissed me. It was all over a disagreement involving another employee that does not bear recounting here.

Sandy and I created a new window company, called Delsan (borrowing the idea from Benada, we took parts of our names MenDEL and SANdy for our new brand).

Delsan became enormously successful, but not without some labor pains.

We needed to lease a factory and had little money with which to do it. I was very fortunate in that the president of Southern Illinois National Bank, who I had met when I was working with Benada, provided me with a $110,000 line of credit.

We started the summer of 1967 with seven people, including Sandy as our bookkeeper. We leased a 10,000-square-foot building at 10447 Midwest Industrial Drive, near Page Boulevard and Ashby road in Overland. It would be four years before Sandy and I could earn enough to pay more than the mortgage and our grocery bills.

Mendel with Stuart and Renee

We were a boutique business going up against big players in the window business, including my former employer. But we were good at what we did and were innovative.

By 1982, we were able to expand to a 44,000 square-foot facility not far away at 1644 Lotsie Road, financed by $1.3 million in St. County industrial revenue bonds. Four years later, we expanded the facility to 67,000 square feet with 100 employees, which by then included my son, Stuart and my son-in-law, Sam Silverstein. Stuart and Sam made a great team. Stuart supervised the production side and Sam handled sales. Our gross revenues topped $6 million.

1982 was the year that I was recognized as Missouri's Small Business Person of the Year, and not long after I received national recognition for my accomplishments that included a visit to the White House and a handshake with President George H.W. Bush. I was also honored to serve as the national president of the American Architectural Manufacturers Association.

I jumped into civic life with both feet. I served as president of my congregation Shaare Zedek and served on the board of directors for the Jewish Center for the Aged and the Anti-Defamation League.

I was flattered to get some nice publicity in the local press, and some of the articles mentioned that I was a Holocaust survivor. But this wasn't something that I wore on my sleeve. I was proud of my business accomplishments and didn't want my past to get in the way of my future. I

Mendel with son, Stuart, at left and Sam Silverstein on right

*Mendel receiving an honor from
then-Governor John Ashcroft of Missouri*

wanted to be appreciated for my acumen and seen as a thriver,
not a survivor.

With that said, I think my Holocaust experience informed
the way I went about my business particularly when it came
to my employees. Of course, I had had the worst kind of work
experience ever invented. I had been a slave laborer during
the war.

Treating my workers appropriately, ethically and
generously meant a lot to me. I started a profit-sharing plan
for every full-time member of our staff and we all did well
together as our company grew.

I remember when we sold the business one of our secretaries was able to leave with a profit-sharing check for nearly $150,000.

I reached a turning point in 1996. I suffered a heart attack. I fully recovered, but it made me take stock and think about what I wanted to do with the rest of my life. By this time I had accumulated some wealth and could easily afford to step back. At the same time, I wanted to continue to serve my community and show my appreciation for what the American experience had provided me and my loved ones.

It had taken me awhile to come around to the idea that I could leave a mark by sharing my Holocaust experience. While I hadn't spoken of this to business associates or even very much to my son and daughter, I had at the urging of a friend, Don Shaikewitz, begun speaking to school groups The first time was in 1978 at Temple Israel in Creve Coeur, less than a mile from where I live.

My daughter, Renee, then a freshman in college, got wind of this and she was incredulous. "You've never told me very much about your experiences and now you're telling your story to a bunch of kids," she said. "What gives?"

I told her that somehow it was easier to tell a bunch of strangers my story. But over the next several months I did share my story with Renee and also Stuart, who was then a junior in high school, and I'm glad I did.

In June of 1985, I sat down with Vida Prince for a lengthy interview for the Oral History Project of the St. Louis Center for Holocaust Studies. The transcript runs nearly 40 pages.

I participated in several other oral history projects and, even more importantly, played a role in helping to establish the Holocaust Museum & Learning Center in west St. Louis County, now close to 25 years old.

Along with visiting schools, I now speak to groups at the center several times each month. I enjoy sharing my stories. The repetition makes the memories somehow less painful for me and the interesting questions that I get makes each encounter unique.

Sandra and I have also endowed a Sunday afternoon film series dedicated to Holocaust remembrance. Along with the movie, we host a post-screening discussion facilitated by an eminent scholar.

Mendel and Sandy, with their children, grandchildren and great-grandchildren.

Mendel and Sandy Rosenberg 1979

9

Legacy

A s I am preparing this text, I have just passed my 90th birthday.

I have to believe God has a purpose for me still being here and having been allowed to come so far.

In 1997, I gave an oral interview in which my family members also participated. There were 12 of us then including grandchildren (and now many more). Everyone got a chance to say something about the experiences that I shared, and their remarks were so meaningful to me. My grandson Geoffrey, then 13, perhaps summed it up most succinctly.

"I am glad he survived," Geoffrey told the interviewer, "because I am here."

Being here is God's gift, I believe, and we all are obligated to make the most of it by being in service to others. That will translate differently for each of us, but in my case it has come down to sharing my experience and encouraging people to learn lessons from it.

The first is the importance of your own family.

Sometimes people tell me they can't get along with their father, mother, brother or sister. I lost my father when I was 13 and my brother when I was 16. And in my formative years as a young adult, I became an orphan, losing my mother before she could see me married or enjoy her grandchildren. I know in my heart how much richer my life could have been if I had my parents and my sibling as long as most Americans get to have them these days. I wonder about people who can't get along with their parents and other family members.

The second lesson that I share is to treat others as you would want to be treated. I am well aware of the other side of that coin. I have seen how well-educated, well-off people, who should know better, can gradually lose their grip on decency and learn to justify cruel measures against their fellow human beings. I have always tried to treat people fairly. When I have, the rewards for having done so always come back to me ten-fold.

As you have read, I wanted to put my past behind me. I have learned that is simply impossible. The past has a way of repeating itself. Today I see how many of my fellow citizens are treating minorities and immigrants in inhumane and irresponsible ways. They have forgotten the stories of their own families. We are a nation of immigrants. This is what makes America great.

Accordingly, I tell people at my remembrance events to wake up to what is going on around them and not to be taken in by people who want to divide us for their own self-interest.

And finally, I encourage everyone, most particularly young people, to never take for granted what this country has to offer. We do live in a land of opportunity as imperfect as it may be. As I tell young people, it is important to be kind and considerate of others. I also encourage them to learn to do things on their own and not to be dependent on someone else. In America, you are in charge of your destiny.

In our faith, we've a saying when someone dies: *May his (or her) memory be a blessing.* I intend to live as long and to be as active as I can well beyond the telling of this tale.

In the meantime, I want the memories I have shared here to be a blessing to you.

Mendel Rosenberg visits with students at the Holocaust Museum & Learning Center in Creve Coeur, Mo.

Photo courtesy of the Holocaust Museum & Learning Center.

Made in the USA
San Bernardino, CA
06 March 2019